LAUGH OUT LOUD DOGS

WENDY PIRK

iThink Books

The Dog Family

You'd never know it by looking at them, but all domesticated dogs, from the biggest to the smallest, came from the grey wolf.

Domestic dogs are tame dogs that live with people as pets. They are members of the canine family.

Q. What does a dog call his father?

A. Paw.

The theory is that thousands of years ago, wolves stole bones and other scraps from around human settlements. The people realized having wolves around kept other large predators away. They started feeding the wolves to make them tame. The tame wolves then became pets.

Close Cousins

Domestic dogs are a subspecies of the grey wolf.

Q. What do you call a silly dog in Australia?

A. A dingo-ling!

The dingo, the wild dog of Australia, is also a subspecies of the wolf.

The coyote is not the same species as the wolf, but it is closely related. Coyotes, wolves and dogs can breed with each other. If a dog and wolf have pups together, the pups are called wolfdogs. If a dog and a coyote have pups together, the pups are coydogs.

The maned wolf is sometimes called "a fox on stilts," because it looks like a fox with really long legs.

Its legs are long so it can see over the tall grass in the savannas of South America, where it lives.

More Distant Cousins

The fennec fox is the smallest wild member of the canine family. It lives in Africa.

This tiny fox has huge ears. They are about half the size of its body.

The raccoon dog lives in Asia and eastern Europe. It is the only dog that hibernates.

Q. What did the wolf say when someone stepped on his foot?

A. Aoooooowwwww!

The tallest breed is the Irish Wolfhound. They look more like ponies than dogs. These dogs are known as "gentle giants," but they were originally bred as war dogs to pull enemy warriors off horses' backs.

Largest Breeds

The Great Dane is a close second to the Wolfhound for world's tallest dog. This breed is thought to be a mix of Irish Wolfhound and mastiff and maybe even greyhound. It is originally from Germany, where it was used to hunt wild boars.

The **English mastiff** is not the tallest dog, but it is the heaviest. These enormous dogs were bred as guard dogs, but they also fought in wars. Their ancestors fought gladiators and wild animals in the Coliseum in ancient Rome.

Q. What do you do when an Irish Wolfhound is sleeping in your bed?

A. Go sleep on the couch.

The **St. Bernard** is another of the world's largest and heaviest dogs. This breed comes from the Alps of France and Switzerland. These rescue dogs found people lost in the snow. They would lay on them to keep them warm until help arrived.

Smallest Breeds

The **Chihuahua** is the smallest dog breed, but even if you told him that, he wouldn't believe you. In his mind, he is probably the size of a wolfhound and isn't afraid to take on dogs far bigger than him.

Q. What did the Chihuahua say to the flea?

A. Stop bugging me!

The Yorkshire Terrier, or Yorkie, is another tiny breed. It is about as tall as a banana is long, and it weighs about the same as a bag of sugar.

Yorkies do not shed. If it is not cut, their hair just keeps growing. It can grow so long that it trips them.

The Pomeranian looks like a cute, fluffy fox, but it is closely related to some common sled dogs, like the American Eskimo dog and the Siberian husky. Pomeranians in the past were much larger than the dogs we see today.

Fastest Breeds

The Greyhound is the fastest dog, but it can't run for a long time. Think of it as the cheetah of the dog world. It has bursts of speed but little stamina and must rest for a long time after it runs.

People think because they are so fast, Greyhounds must have lots of energy and need a lot of exercise. Not so. Greyhounds are naturally quite lazy and are perfectly happy to sprawl out and relax on the couch.

The Saluki is one of the oldest dog breeds. It is not as fast as the greyhound but can run for long distances.

Q. Why did the Whippet cross the road twice?

A. He was trying to fetch a boomerang.

The Whippet looks like a mini greyhound. It is the fastest runner for a dog of its size. It is can make sharp turns as it runs at top speed and is great at catching Frisbees.

Q. Why did the dog stay in the shade?

A. Because he didn't want to turn into a hot dog!

A hairless dog is not always completely hairless. It can have hair on its head, feet and tail. Its bare skin needs to be protected from the sun or it will burn.

The Chinese Crested has both a hairless and furred type. The furred dogs are called powder puffs.

The gene that causes hairlessness also affects the dogs' teeth. Many Chinese Crested dogs have crooked or missing teeth.

Hairless Breeds

The Peruvian Inca Orchid is the national dog of Peru. The Inca believed it had special healing powers because its body was so warm.

This dog's job was carrying messages between different Inca settlements.

Unique Breeds

The Chinese Shar Pei might look cute and a bit silly with its wrinkly skin, but it was bred to be a hunting and fighting dog. The loose folds of its skin are thick and rough like sandpaper. They protect the dog in a fight. If an opponent bites the Shar Pei, the opponent gets a mouthful of skin instead of bone, muscle or other important body parts.

Q. What did the dog say when she sat on a sheet of sandpaper?

A. Rough! Rough!

It might look like an oversized mop, but a medium-sized dog is under all that fur. The Puli is a herding dog from Hungary. As its fur grows, it curls into long cords that look like dreadlocks.

Norwegian Lundehund was bred to hunt puffins in their nests, high on rocky cliffs. This dog has 6 toes on each foot and is an excellent climber. It is also super flexible. Its head can bend all the way back to touch its spine.

Dogs are grouped into 7 different categories depending what job they were bred to do.

The groups are:
• working dogs
• herding dogs
• sporting dogs
• hounds
• terriers
• toy or companion dogs
• non-sporting dogs.

Q. What type of dog is best at telling time?

A. A watch dog!

Types of Dogs

Working Dogs

The Bull Mastiff is a guard dog.

Dogs in the working dog group, like the Bull Mastiff and the Newfoundland dog, were bred to help people. Dogs in this group are powerful. They include guard dogs, rescue dogs and sled dogs.

The Newfoundland dog is an excellent swimmer and can save people from drowning.

Herding and Sporting Dogs

Herding dogs were bred to herd or round up livestock like cattle or sheep.

The Border Collie is one of the best herding dogs. It is very smart and loves to work.

The Corgi is a "heeler," meaning that it nips cattle in the heels to get them to move where it wants them to go. The Corgi's short legs keep it low to the ground and out of the way of a kicking cow's hooves.

Q. What do you get when you cross a sheepdog with a rose?
A. A collie-flower!

Sporting dogs, also called gun dogs, were bred to hunt game birds.

Pointers sniff out where a bird is hiding and point at the spot for the hunter.

Retrievers, like the Golden Retriever, were bred to find a downed bird and bring it back to the hunter. They will happily find and bring you anything you train them to.

Dogs in the hound group are split into 2 types, scenthounds and sighthounds. Scenthounds use their sense of smell to track prey. Sighthounds use their eyesight and speed to spot prey and chase it down.

The Bloodhound is perhaps the most famous scenthound and has the best sense of smell of all dogs.

The Scottish Deerhound is a sighthound. It was considered the royal dog of Scotland because only noblemen were allowed to own one. It was bred to hunt deer but also hunted wolves and wild boar.

Hounds and Terriers

Terriers were bred to hunt animals that people considered to be pests.

Small Terriers like the West Highland White Terrier, could follow small animals into their underground burrows to catch them.

The Bull Terrier is a cross between a bulldog and a terrier. It was bred for dog fighting but turned out to be much better at chasing rats. Bull Terriers are often called the clowns of the dog world because they are so playful.

Q. What kind of pet does Dracula have?

A. A Bloodhound!

Toy and Non-sporting Dogs

Dogs in the toy or companion group were bred to be lapdogs or pampered pets.

The Pug originally came from China, where it was a favorite pet of emperors.

Because it has smooshed in face and bulgy eyes, you can actually pop out a Pug's eyes if you squeeze its neck too hard.

The Papillon is known for its big, butterfly-shaped ears.

Non-sporting dogs are the breeds that don't really fit in any of the other groups.

Another Chinese breed, the Chow Chow is born with a pink tongue that darkens to bluish black by the time the dog is an adult.

Q. What do you get if you cross a Cocker Spaniel, a Poodle and a rooster?

A. A cockerpoodle doo!

Poodles are one of the cleverest dog breeds. It is probably the silly haircut that makes people think these dogs are not smart.

A dog's hearing is about 4 times better than ours. They can hear high-pitched sounds that our ears miss. They can also hear sounds that are farther away.

Q. What do you call a dog wearing earphones?

A. Anything you want to. He can't hear you.

Ears

Dogs ears can be either erect or pendant. Erect ears stand up straight on the head. Pendant ears are floppy and hang down.

Some breeds, like the Dalmatian, are more likely to be born deaf. The same thing that gives the dogs their black and white coat can also make them deaf. About one-third of all Dalmatians cannot hear out of one or both ears.

Q: Why did the Dalmatian go to the eye doctor?

A: He was seeing spots.

Eyes

Dogs are not colour blind, but they cannot see colour the way we do. They see the world in shades of grey, blue and yellow. They cannot see green or red.

Dogs can have two different eye colours. It is more common in huskies and Australian Shepherds than in other breeds. Melanin, the stuff that makes your skin tan in the sun, gives the iris of the eye its colour. If one iris has more melanin than the other, it will be darker.

Dogs have 3 eyelids. The third eyelid, called the nictitating membrane or haw, acts much like a windshield wiper, sweeping dirt off the eyeball. You usually can't see it because it is tucked in the inner corner of the dog's eye.

Nose

A dog's nose print is unique, like our fingerprints.

Q; Why is a dog's nose in the middle of its face?

A: Because it is the scenter!

Dogs have a much better sense of smell than humans do. In dogs, the part of the brain that deals with smell is 40 times the size of a human's.

Dogs have about 220 million cells in their nose that pick up smells. Humans have only about 5 million.

Paws

Q. Why can't dogs work the DVD machine?

A. They always hit the "paws" button.

Dogs sweat through their feet. They have sweat glands in their paw pads. When your dog is hot, you may notice that he leaves little sweaty paw prints on the ground when he walks.

A dog's foot has 5 claws. Each toe has a claw, and the fifth claw higher up on the leg, is called a dewclaw. Some dogs have dewclaws only on the front legs, and some have them on all 4 legs.

Dewclaws on the front legs help the dog grip when he is running, especially if he turns quickly. They also help a dog climb and hold onto things like sticks or bones.

A dog's paw has 4 pads. The pads act as cushions for the bones of his feet when he is walking or running.

Some dogs, like the Newfoundland dog have webbed paws, to help them swim.

Communication

Although they do bark and whine, dogs communicate most with their body language.

A dog tells you it wants to play by "bowing." It sticks its butt in the air and straightens its front legs, kind of like the downward dog pose in yoga.

Q. What did the dog say to the tree?
A. Bark.

A yawning dog might not be tired. Yawning is one way dogs let you know they are worried or stressed.

Have you ever wondered why, after your dog pees, she kicks back and scrapes the ground where she just peed? Dogs pee to mark their territory. By scattering the dirt or leaves where she peed, she is making sure other dogs know she is claiming that spot as her own.

Moods

You can tell a lot about your dog just by looking at her.

A happy dog has her head held high, ears up and mouth open. She will usually also wag her tail and may pant.

A scared dog
keeps her body low
to the ground, with her
ears flat against her head
and her tail between her
legs. She will not look
you in the eye.

An angry dog
holds her ears back
and bares her teeth. The fur
on her back stands straight
up, and her tail is held straight.
She will stare straight at you.
Never look an angry dog
in the eye. It could
attack you.

Puppies

When a puppy is born, it is helpless. It can't move, see or hear. Its eyes are closed, and its ears are folded down against its head.

A puppy's eyes open when it is about 2 weeks old. It still can't see properly, though. Everything is still blurry.

Q: What do dogs have that no other animal has?

A: Puppies!

All puppies are born with blue eyes. The eyes change to their adult colour when the puppies are about 12 weeks old.

By the time the puppy is 3 weeks old, its ears have unfolded from against its head, and it can hear.

Newborn puppies spend most of their time curled up together to stay warm. If they get too cold, they can get sick.

Once their eyes are open, puppies are curious to explore the world around them. But they cannot walk yet. They can only crawl on their bellies.

Growing Up

Q. What happened to the dog that had her puppies on the sidewalk?

A. She was ticketed for littering.

A puppy starts trying to stand up when it is about 15 days old. By day 21, it takes its first wobbly steps.

Puppies should not be taken away from their mom until they at least 2 months old. Puppies that stay with mom even longer, at least 3 months, are usually happier and get along better with other dogs and people.

Choosing a Dog

It is exciting to bring a new pup home, but you can't just pick a dog because it is cute. You need to know a bit about its breed. Dogs were bred for different jobs and have different qualities and needs. Choose a dog that suits your home.

Some dogs are good with kids, but some are not. Some need only a small space, and some need an acreage to run around on. Choosing the right dog for your family means you'll have a happy dog. A happy dog makes a good pet.

Unless you want a purebred dog, adoption is best. Animal shelters are bursting with dogs that need good homes.

If you decide on a purebred, look for a respected breeder. That way you can be sure the dog comes from a family of dogs that do not have problems with their behavior or health.

Q. Why can't dogs be good dancers?

A. Because they have two left feet.

Grooming

There are many things you need to do to take good care of your dog.

Brush your dog at least twice a week to keep his coat healthy and tangle free.

If your dog needs a bath, use a shampoo made just for dogs. Regular shampoo can bother your dog's skin.

Q. What kind of dog likes taking a bath?

A. A shampoodle!

As you brush his fur, check you dog for fleas and ticks. Flea and tick bites make your dog itchy and sore. These pests can also carry diseases that can make your dog sick.

Another important part of caring for your dog is keeping his claws trimmed.

If you can hear the claws clicking on the floor as the dog walks, they need trimming.

When claws get too long, they can get caught on things and split, which really hurts. Long claws can also make walking uncomfortable or painful for your pup. They can cut into the pads on his feet.

Teeth and Claws

You'll also need to brush your dog's teeth. Dogs can get cavities and gum disease, just like people can. Make sure you use toothpaste that is specially made for dogs. Regular toothpaste is poisonous to dogs.

You can also feed him dental treats that are made to help keep your dog's teeth clean.

Q: How is a toothless dog like a tree?

A: It is all bark and no bite.

Exercise

All dogs need exercise. A daily walk keeps your dog healthy. It also gives your dog a chance to explore.

Exercise is good for the mind as well as the body. A bored dog is more likely to get into trouble. Something as simple as a game of fetch with a stick or ball keeps your dog's mind busy.

Some more active breeds, like Border Collies and Shelties, need more than a walk or game of fetch. These dogs do really well in agility training to burn off their energy.

Q: What dog can jump higher than a tree?

A: Any dog can jump higher than a tree. Trees can't jump.

If they are left alone too much or do not have enough to keep them busy, dogs can develop bad habits. They might bark too much or destroy your things.

Safe Travel

As your furry BFF, your dog is happy to tag along wherever you go. If you are going out in the car, there are a few things to keep in mind to keep your pup safe.

NEVER leave your dog alone in the car, especially in summer. On a hot day, the inside of the car can get so hot that your dog can die.

Q: What is the fastest dog in the world?

A: A lab-orghini!

It is also not safe to let your dog stick his head out the open window of a moving car. Rocks, dirt and even bugs can hit your dog in the face and damage his eyes. The wind can hurt his ears.

Unsafe Treats

Onion and garlic are toxic to dogs. Even a little can damage their blood cells. If you feed your dog table scraps, watch out for prepared foods that might have onion or garlic in them, like pasta sauces, sausage and deli meats.

Never feed your dog chocolate or candy. Chocolate is poisonous to dogs. They can die if they eat even a small amount. Some candy has a sweetener called xylitol that can make dogs sick.

Q: What is purple and barks?
A: A grape dane!

Caffeine is also bad for dogs, especially small dogs. A few laps of coffee, tea, hot chocolate, pop or an energy drink, might not hurt your pup, but too much can kill her.

Grapes and raisins can also poison your dog. Eating walnuts can give them seizures.

Q: What do dogs eat when they are watching movies?

A: Pupcorn!

Pet stores sell plenty of safe dog treats for your pet. Just because they are safe doesn't mean they are healthy. Think of them as the cookies of the dog world. A "sometimes food," not a daily snack.

Safe Treats

Two of the best foods to give your pup as a treat are cooked chicken and eggs. Make sure there is no salt, pepper or other seasonings on them.

Apple slices and baby carrots are also great choices. They both help clean your dog's teeth. Apple slices also help make a dog's breath smell better.

Dogs love peanut butter!! Make sure it is the natural kind with no added sugar, salt or sweeteners.

They also love yogurt! Again, make sure it does not have added sugar or sweetener, especially not xylitol.

Working Dogs

Because they are so smart and easy to train, dogs are given many different jobs.

Q. Why did the dog cross the road?

A. To catch the chicken.

Guard dogs protect people's property.

Police dogs can chase and catch criminals that are trying to run away.

Sniffer dogs can work for the fire department, the police or the military. They can sniff out weapons, bombs, poisons and other dangerous things.

Sniffer dogs can also find people who are buried by avalanches or buildings that have collapsed, like in an earthquake.

Water rescue dogs are lifeguards. They can save people from drowning.

Service Dogs

Dogs can also be trained to help people. They can be service dogs, companion dogs and therapy dogs.

Service dogs can help guide people who cannot see. They can be the ears for people who cannot hear. They let their owners know if the doorbell rings or if a timer goes off.

Q. What do you call a dog that licks an electrical outlet?

A. Sparky

Companion dogs do the everyday tasks that their owners cannot do. They can close doors, turn on light switches and pick things up that have been dropped.

Medical companion dogs can warn their owners if they are going to have a seizure or if their blood sugar is to low.

Therapy dogs go into hospitals to comfort patients.

BUBBLES

It might seem gross to you, but dogs sniff each other butts to say hello! With a sniff, they can tell if the other is dog is male or female, if it is healthy and even what kind of mood it is in.

Q. Why did the dog refuse to play soccer?

A. It was a boxer.

Random Facts

The Basenji does not bark. It makes a yodeling sound, called a "baroo." Its voice box is shaped differently than that of other dogs.

Dalmation puppies are born white and get their spots as they get older. The black spots are actually on their skin, not just their fur.

Dog Myths

If a dog's nose is warm or dry, he is sick

The temperature of a dog's nose has nothing to do with his health. It changes throughout the day. It might be warm when he first wakes up and cool a few hours later.

A dog can still be sick even if he has a wet nose. Often dog's noses are wet because the dogs lick them. Also, some dogs just have wetter noses than others. So drier doesn't mean sick, and wetter doesn't mean healthy. You'll need to look at the whole dog to see if he is healthy, not just his nose.

A wagging tail means a dog is happy

Not always. Dogs do wag their tails when they are happy. A nervous dog might also wag its tail. Look for other body language clues to see if the dog is happy or not.

Some research suggests that the direction the tail wags offers a clue to how the dog is feeling. A tail that starts wagging to the right means the dog is happy. A tail that starts wagging to the left means the dog wants some space.

Q. What is a sick dog called?

A. A germy shepherd.

The Publisher: iThink Books

iThink Books is an imprint of Folklore Publishing Ltd.
www.folklorepublishing.com

Library and Archives Canada Cataloguing in Publication

Pirk, Wendy, 1973–, author
    Laugh out loud: dogs / Wendy Pirk.

ISBN 978-1-897206-15-7 (softcover)

    1. Dogs—Juvenile humor. 2. Dogs—Miscellanea—Juvenile literature. 3. Canadian wit and humor (English)—Juvenile literature. 4. Wit and humor, Juvenile. I. Title. II. Title: Dogs.

PN6231.D68P57 2018   jC818'.602   C2017-906355-3

Front cover credits: TheDogPhotographer/Thinkstock.

Back cover credits: CaptureLight/Thinkstock; TAGSTOCK1/Thinkstock; DeRepente/Thinkstock.

Photo credits: Every effort has been made to accurately credit the sources of photographs and illustrations. Any errors or omissions should be reported directly to the publisher for correction in future editions. *From Thinkstock:* Alona Rjabceva, 41; AlonsoAguilar, 44b; anuta-shadow, 11; AvanHeertum, 49a; Azaliya, 23b; Bagicat, 34; Bigandt_Photography, 18; BilevichOlga, 27; burhan21, 48b; CaptureLight, 8a, 17b; castenoid, 39; Chris Amaral, 22a; cynoclub, 9b; damedeeso, 48a, 62; Darren Brown, 22b; DeRepente, 32; dimarik, 45c; djiledesign, 16; DoraZett, 61b; EcoPic, 12a; elementals, 60; Elen11, 40, 56; estt, 3; f8grapher, 19a; FluxFactory, 35b; fongleon356, 24a; forisana, 9a; GlobalP, 13b; gorodisskij, 20b; Gschwald, 7a; Helioscribe, 49b; hkuchera, 4; huettenhoelscher, 47a; Huntstock, 59a; Ingram Publishing, 29; irisphoto2, 25a; janpla01, 15; johan63, 54; Kane Skennar, 63; KateLeigh, 20a; Kerkez, 52; kosziv, 51; kozorog, 31; KPGS, 28; Laitho, 25b; lariko3, 12b; Laures, 35a; Lindsay_Helms, 26; Madjuszka, 61a; manukaphoto, 50; Maximillian100, 55; Mike Watson Images, 2; MirasWonderland, 7b; Mitsou Tamaki, 10; monkeybusinessimages, 53, 59b; morrbyte, 11a; MoustacheGirl, 43; Musat, 6; OldFulica, 5b; oleghz, 37a; onetouchspark, 13a; PavelRodimov, 46; Photodisc, 21b; photosbyjim, 57a; RalfWeigel, 8b; rangreiss, 44a; sanjagrujic, 36; Sephirot17, 57b; Sergey Lavrentev, 24b; Srisakorn, 45b; sssss1gmel, 17a; SVproduction, 38; tayfoon, 19b; ThamKC, 45a; timalfordphoto, 21; tsik, 23a; vaaltonen, 42; Valeria Vechterova, 47b; vindicta76, 56a; Volodymyr_Plysiuk, 37b; Wavetop, 33; Whitepointer, 5a; WiindWolfPhotography, 30; XiXinXing, 58; Zuzule, 14.

Animal Illustrations: julos/Thinkstock.

We acknowledge the financial support of the Government of Canada.
Nous reconnaissons l'appui financier du gouvernement du Canada.

Funded by the Government of Canada
Financé par le gouvernement du Canada | **Canadä**

Produced with the assistance of the Government of Alberta.

Government

PC: 38-3